PATRICK MAH S

Making a Difference as a Football MVP

By Katie Kawa

People Who Make a Difference

KidHaven
PUBLISHING

Published in 2025 by
KidHaven Publishing, an Imprint of Greenhaven Publishing, LLC
2544 Clinton St.
Buffalo, NY 14224

Designer: Deanna Lepovich
Editor: Katie Kawa

Photo credits: Cover All-Pro Reels/Flickr; p. 5 European Sports Photo Agency/Alamy Stock Photo; p. 7 DFree/Shutterstock.com; pp. 9, 20 Zuma Press, Inc./Alamy Stock Photo; pp. 11, 13, 15, 18 UPI/Alamy Stock Photo; p. 17 Cal Sport Media/Alamy Stock Photo; p. 21 T.Sumaetho/Shutterstock.com.

Library of Congress Cataloging-in-Publication Data

Names: Kawa, Katie, author.
Title: Patrick Mahomes : making a difference as a football MVP / Katie Kawa.
Description: Buffalo, New York : KidHaven Publishing, [2025] | Series: People who make a difference | Includes index.
Identifiers: LCCN 2024010647 | ISBN 9781534548015 (library binding) | ISBN 9781534548008 (paperback) | ISBN 9781534548022 (ebook)
Subjects: LCSH: Mahomes, Patrick, 1995–Juvenile literature. | Kansas City Chiefs (Football team)–Juvenile literature. | Quarterbacks (Football)–United States–Biography–Juvenile literature. | Football players–United States–Biography–Juvenile literature.
Classification: LCC GV939.M284 K39 2025 | DDC 796.332092 [B]–dc23/eng/20240307
LC record available at https://lccn.loc.gov/2024010647

Printed in the United States of America

Find us on

CONTENTS

The Most Valuable Player 4

Growing Up Around Sports 6

Trying Two Sports 8

A Rising Star 10

Super Bowl Superstar 12

Back in the Big Game 14

Helping Kids 16

Taking a Stand 18

A Role Model 20

Glossary 22

For More Information 23

Index 24

THE MOST VALUABLE PLAYER

What does it mean to be the MVP? It means you're the Most Valuable Player—the player who makes the biggest difference! Patrick Mahomes knows all about what it takes to be the MVP. He's been named the MVP of the National Football League (NFL) and the MVP of the Super Bowl, which is the NFL's **championship**. This shows that Patrick makes a big difference every time he steps on the football field.

Patrick also makes a big difference off the field. From helping kids succeed to speaking out against **racism**, he's doing valuable things in his community too.

In His Words

"I want to always be remembered as a great quarterback, but remembered more as a better person."

— Interview for *CBS Mornings* TV show from July 2023

Patrick Mahomes has become a star in the NFL playing quarterback for the Kansas City Chiefs. A quarterback's main job is to get the ball to other players so they can score touchdowns. Patrick helps people succeed on and off the field!

GROWING UP AROUND SPORTS

Patrick grew up around **professional** sports, but he didn't dream of playing in the NFL. Instead, he spent his childhood wanting to play professional baseball like his dad. When Patrick Lavon Mahomes II was born on September 17, 1995, his dad was a Major League Baseball (MLB) pitcher. Patrick and his younger brother Jackson visited their dad at work and enjoyed spending time around him and the other MLB players.

Patrick played a lot of sports in and around Tyler, Texas, which is where he was born. He especially loved baseball, basketball, and football.

In His Words

"I'm proud to be Black. And I'm proud to have a white mom too. I'm just proud of who I am. And I've always had that confidence [belief] in myself."

— Interview with GQ magazine from July 2020

Patrick's dad is Black, and his mom is white. Being biracial—having parents of two different races—is part of who Patrick is, and he's spoken openly about being proud of everything that makes him who he is.

TRYING TWO SPORTS

Patrick kept playing baseball, basketball, and football at Whitehouse High School in Whitehouse, Texas. He then decided that he wanted to keep playing baseball and football after high school. Texas Tech University gave Patrick the chance to do that, and he started school there in 2014.

During his first two years at Texas Tech, Patrick played in baseball games as a pitcher and a hitter and in football games as a quarterback. Then, in 2016, Patrick announced that he was going to stop playing baseball so he could **focus** on football. That season, Patrick had more passing yards and total touchdowns than any other college quarterback!

In His Words

"So much of what I do is because I played baseball."

— Interview with *Esquire* magazine from October 2023

8

Patrick could have played professional baseball like his dad. He was drafted, or chosen, by the Detroit Tigers in the 2014 MLB draft. However, he decided to follow the path to the NFL instead.

A RISING STAR

By 2017, Patrick was ready for the NFL. That year, the Kansas City Chiefs chose Patrick with the 10th pick in the NFL draft. In December 2017, Patrick started his first game for the Chiefs, and he led the team to a win!

The wins kept coming after that. In 2018, Patrick took over as the starting quarterback for the Chiefs. That season, he recorded 50 touchdowns and was named the NFL MVP—an honor he was given in early 2019. In January 2019, Patrick led the Chiefs to their first **playoff** win at home since 1993—and he was just getting started.

In His Words

"I want to be someone that the kids can look up to and say that, 'Hey, I want to be like Patrick Mahomes.' ... And I want parents to think that, 'Hey, that's a guy that I want my kid to be like.'"

— Interview for *CBS Mornings* TV show from July 2023

Patrick is shown here warming up before a home game at Arrowhead Stadium in Kansas City, Missouri. Although he didn't lead the Chiefs to a championship in 2019, Super Bowl success was right around the corner.

SUPER BOWL SUPERSTAR

After losing in the playoffs in 2019, Patrick worked hard to make sure that didn't happen the next season. His hard work paid off! The Chiefs won the **AFC Championship** in 2020, which sent them to Super Bowl LIV. They beat the San Francisco 49ers to become Super Bowl champions. Patrick was also named Super Bowl MVP.

Patrick and the Chiefs won another AFC Championship in 2021, but they lost the Super Bowl that year to the Tampa Bay Buccaneers. They made their way back to the Super Bowl in 2023, and they beat the Philadelphia Eagles to become champions once again.

In His Words

"That's how I'll play the game. I try to enjoy it. I try to enjoy my time with my family. And when I'm on TV or when I'm in the spotlight, I try to show off the right example."

— Interview for
CBS Mornings TV show
from July 2023

In 2023, Patrick was named Super Bowl MVP and NFL MVP!

BACK IN THE BIG GAME

In 2024, Patrick led the Chiefs back to the Super Bowl, and they faced the 49ers again. The game was tied at the end of the fourth quarter, so it went to **overtime**. Patrick threw a touchdown pass in overtime, so the Chiefs won! Patrick was named Super Bowl MVP for the third time.

It was a happy time for Chiefs fans. However, happiness turned to sadness when one person was killed and others were hurt in a shooting during a Super Bowl **celebration** in Kansas City. Patrick went to the hospital to visit kids who were hurt that day.

In His Words

"It's the start … we're not done. I know we're going to celebrate tonight, but we got a young team; we [are] going to keep this thing going."

— Speech after being named Super Bowl MVP in 2024

Patrick and his teammates, including Travis Kelce (shown here), care a lot about their fans, who are sometimes called Chiefs Kingdom.

15

HELPING KIDS

Visiting kids in the hospital isn't the only way Patrick helps people. In 2019, Patrick started the 15 and the Mahomies Foundation. This is an organization, or group, that helps kids in different ways.

For example, the foundation's Read for 15 **program** invites kids to read for at least 15 minutes a day for 15 weeks. Patrick helped start the **Volunteer** for 15 program that calls on kids to spend 15 hours volunteering. He's also helped give more than $4 million to support programs that provide kids with glasses, school supplies, safe playgrounds, and more.

In His Words

"It's a foundation that is designed [planned] around all kids—kids that don't get the same opportunities that I had … or kids that are in the hospital … Those kids are the ones that train harder than me by a hundred times every single day, and I want to make sure I can give back to them."

— Interview for *The Tonight Show Starring Jimmy Fallon* from April 2019

Helping kids became even more important to Patrick after he became a dad. He met his wife, Brittany, in high school. In 2021, Brittany gave birth to their daughter, Sterling. In 2022, their son, Patrick (who's known as Bronze), was born.

TAKING A STAND

Patrick wants to make sure all kids have a bright future. One way he's fighting for this is by using his voice to speak out against racism. In 2020, Patrick teamed up with other Black NFL players to make a video. In this video, they pushed the NFL to take a strong stand against racism.

Patrick also understands that voting helps us shape our future as a country. He's worked with teammates to help people register, or sign up, to vote in Kansas City. He's also supported basketball superstar LeBron James's efforts to get people to vote.

In His Words

"I understand my **platform** ... Sometimes it's not about money. It's not about fame. It's about doing what's right."

— Interview with *GQ* magazine from July 2020

18

The Life of Patrick Mahomes

1995
Patrick Mahomes II is born on September 17 in Tyler, Texas.

2014
Patrick is chosen by the Detroit Tigers in the MLB draft, but he begins college at Texas Tech University.

2016
Patrick stops playing college baseball to focus on football.

2017
Patrick is drafted by the NFL's Kansas City Chiefs and plays in his first NFL game.

2018
Patrick becomes the starting quarterback for the Chiefs.

2019
Patrick is named NFL MVP and starts the 15 and the Mahomies Foundation.

2020
The Chiefs win the Super Bowl, and Patrick is named Super Bowl MVP.

2021
Patrick's daughter, Sterling, is born.

2022
Patrick marries Brittany Matthews (now Brittany Mahomes), and she gives birth to their son, Patrick "Bronze" Mahomes.

2023
The Chiefs win the Super Bowl, Patrick is named NFL MVP and Super Bowl MVP, and he appears in the Netflix show *Quarterback*.

2024
Patrick wins his third Super Bowl and third Super Bowl MVP title.

The life of Patrick Mahomes has been filled with football success!

A ROLE MODEL

Patrick's Super Bowl wins have helped him become a superstar! He's been on TV in commercials, or ads, and as part of the Netflix show *Quarterback*, which came out in 2023. He's one of the NFL's most famous faces.

Patrick knows how to use his fame to help others. He wants to be a good role model—someone kids can look up to. Whether he's opening a new playground, spending time with kids who are sick, or speaking out against racism, he's doing his part to make a difference and to **inspire** others to make a difference too.

In His Words

"I want people to see the love that I have for the game of football, the love I have for my family, and the love I have for being a role model. And I think if they see that, and they remember me as that, then I've done what I need to do."

— Interview for *CBS Mornings* TV show from July 2023

Be Like
Patrick Mahomes!

Volunteer with a group that helps kids in need.

Raise money for groups that help kids in your community.

Remind the adults in your life to vote, and go with them when they do to learn more about how voting works.

Make cards for kids who are in a local hospital.

If you play sports, be a good teammate.

Talk to your friends and family members about racism and ways you can take a stand against it.

Work hard in school and in sports or other activities you're part of.

If someone you know is sick or hurt and in the hospital, visit them to cheer them up.

These are just some ways you can be like Patrick Mahomes and become the MVP in your community!

GLOSSARY

AFC Championship: A contest held every year to decide which is the best team in the American Football Conference (AFC)—a group made up of half the teams in the NFL.

celebration: Something special or fun, such as a big gathering, that is done in honor of an important event.

championship: A contest to find out who's the best team in a sport.

focus: To direct attention or effort at something.

inspire: To move someone to do something great.

overtime: Extra time added to the end of a sporting event.

platform: An opportunity to talk publicly.

playoff: Relating to a series of games played after the regular season of a sport is over to find out who the best team is that season.

professional: Having to do with a job someone does for a living.

program: A plan under which action may be taken toward a goal.

racism: The practice of treating others poorly because they are part of a different race, or group of people who look alike in certain ways. This word also relates to governments and societies that allow one race to be treated better than others.

volunteer: To do something to help because you want to do it.

FOR MORE INFORMATION

WEBSITES

15 and the Mahomies Foundation

www.15andthemahomies.org

The official website of Patrick's foundation has stories about the work the foundation is doing to help kids.

NFL.com: Patrick Mahomes

www.nfl.com/players/patrick-mahomes

Patrick's page on the official NFL website has facts, news stories, and videos about him.

BOOKS

Corso, Phil. *Patrick Mahomes.* Buffalo, NY: PowerKids Press, 2022.

Greenberg, Keith Elliot. *Patrick Mahomes vs. Peyton Manning: Who Would Win?* Minneapolis, MN: Lerner Publications, 2024.

Morey, Allan. *Patrick Mahomes.* Minneapolis, MN: Bellwether Media, 2023.

INDEX

A
AFC Championship, 12

B
baseball, 6, 8, 9, 19
basketball, 6, 8, 18

C
children, 17, 19

D
draft, 9, 10, 19

F
15 and the Mahomies Foundation, 16, 19

J
James, LeBron, 18

K
Kelce, Travis, 15

M
Mahomes, Brittany, 17, 19

N
NFL MVP, 4, 10, 13, 19

P
parents, 6, 7, 9
playoffs, 10, 12

Q
Quarterback (TV show), 19, 20

R
racism, 4, 18, 20, 21

S
Super Bowl MVP, 4, 12, 13, 14, 19

T
Texas Tech University, 8, 19
touchdowns, 5, 8, 10, 14

V
voting, 18, 21